W0298678

Tom Dahlke & Jan Birck

Englisch mit Rätseln und Witzen

moses.

My name is Fredy Fox

I am many years old.

My address is: Forest Drive 007

Pinewood Springs

My telephone number is 689771

My favourite colour is green

My best friend's name is

Brian Bear

My favourite food is chocolate

and more chocolate

My favourite drink is

banana milk-shake

My favourite sport is

baseball

Jetzt bist du an der Reihe! Male oder klebe ein Bild von dir in das Kästchen!

Words, words, words

Diese Wörter kennst du bestimmt schon! Deute auf die Tiere und Dinge und sprich dazu, z. B.: "I can see a table."

Hier findest du die passenden Wörter:
fox, apple, flower, sun, car, plane, door, satchel, window, fish, tree, ruler, dog, elephant, cow, table, bike, house, chair, ice cream, ball, mouse, pencil, cup.

English names

Im Buchstabengitter sind 13 Vornamen versteckt.
Kreise sie bitte ein!
Schreibe dann die Namen der Tiere fertig!

J _ _ _

C _ _ _ _ _

R _ _ _

S _ L _ _

R _ _ _ _ _ _

S _ M _ _

Y	J	O	H	N	N	Y	O	U	A
R	R	S	C	H	A	R	L	Y	E
I	J	A	T	R	I	T	A	B	F
C	A	M	S	A	L	L	Y	O	R
H	N	M	A	L	A	N	E	B	E
A	E	Y	R	M	A	R	Y	B	D
R	R	I	N	A	N	C	Y	Y	D
D	B	R	I	A	N	F	I	C	Y

BR _ _ _

N _ _ _ _

M _ _ _

A _ _ _

F _ _ _ _ _

BO _ _ _

J _ _ _ _ _

Schreibe jetzt alle übriggebliebenen Buchstaben aus dem Gitter der Reihe nach in diese Kästchen:

!

Parts of the body

Ordne die Wörter den Körperteilen zu!

Auge	eye	Hand	hand	Bein	leg
Nase	nose	Schulter	shoulder	Knie	knee
Mund	mouth	Arm	arm	Fuß	foot
Ohr	ear	Finger	finger	Zehe	toe
Hals	neck	Ellbogen	elbow	Haare	hair

What's missing?

Write what is missing!
Then draw in what's missing in each picture!

What's that in German?

Diese Wörter kannst du bestimmt schon übersetzen. Schreibe die deutschen Wörter in die Fahnen.

Trage bitte bei jedem Bild die Nummer der passenden Wortfahne ein!

It's raining nouns

Colour each word that names a person (boy, girl, …) red!
Colour each word that names an animal (cat, …) blue!
Colour each word that names a thing (car, …) green!

Numbers

Verbinde was zusammengehört!

1	three	
2	five	
3	one	
4	two	
5	four	
6	seven	
7	nine	
8	six	
9	ten	
10	eight	

Trage die Zahlen in die Kästchen ein!

1	one	2		3		4		5	
6		7		8		9		10	

Join the numbers

Verbinde die Punkte in der richtigen Zahlenreihenfolge!

What‘s the order?

first second third fourth fifth sixth seventh eight ninth tenth

Ergänze die fehlenden Wörter!

☆ The dog is fourth .

☆ The giraffe is ____________ .

☆ Freddy, the fox, is ____________ .

☆ The ____________ is eight .

☆ The elephant is ____________.

☆ The cow is ____________.

☆ The ____________ is ninth.

☆ Brian, the bear, is ____________ .

☆ The cat is ____________.

☆ Charly, the frog, is ____________.

What is the opposite of "not in"?

Most people will answer " out" !But think again! The opposite of " not in" is "in" .

Hungry Fox

Freddy Fuchs träumt vom Essen.

Can you make the words?

fish ______ ______

______ ______

______ ______

______ ______

______ ______

Starts the same?

Schau die beiden Bilder in jedem Kästchen genau an! Kreuze das Kästchen an, wenn beide Begriffe mit dem gleichen Buchstaben beginnen!

"a" or "an"?

a duck

an astronaut

Ausnahmen:

a uniform
a unit
a unicorn
an hour

Letter salad

Unscramble the words and connect them with the pictures!

Wenn du alles richtig gemacht hast, bleibt ein Buchstabenkästchen übrig. Setze auch dieses Wort zusammen und male ein passendes Bild auf Freddys Schild!

At home

Read the sentences about the house. Write "yes" or "no" in the boxes!

Freddy and Charly Frog are in the kitchen.	yes
Charly Frog is eating a sandwich.	
The cat is sleeping.	
The cat is watching TV.	
A car is in the garage.	
Miss Mouse is sitting on the table.	
A bird is on the roof.	
Freddy is cooking.	
Emmy Duck is in the bathroom.	
There are four chairs in the kitchen.	
	5x yes / 5x no

Who is who?

Lies jede Angabe sorgfältig und verbinde sie mit der passenden Person!

cook

tourist

taxi-driver

grandfather

A person who cooks the meals in a restaurant is a ....

You see him, when you are ill. It's the ....

A very young child is a ....

Your mother's father is your ....

A person who drives a taxi is a ....

A person you really like is your ....

The person who brings the letters is a ....

A person who goes sightseeing in a town is a ....

baby

doctor

friend

postman

Freddy's kitchen

Beantworte bitte die Fragen!

Where is the cat? ______________________________

Where is the snake? ______________________________

Where is the mouse? ______________________________

Suche diese Dinge im Buchstabengitter und kreise sie ein!

p	i	c	t	u	r	e	c
t	u	r	t	l	e	b	u
t	c	s	i	n	k	o	r
a	h	f	o	r	k	t	t
b	a	v	a	s	e	t	a
l	i	c	a	k	e	l	i
e	r	e	g	g	c	e	n

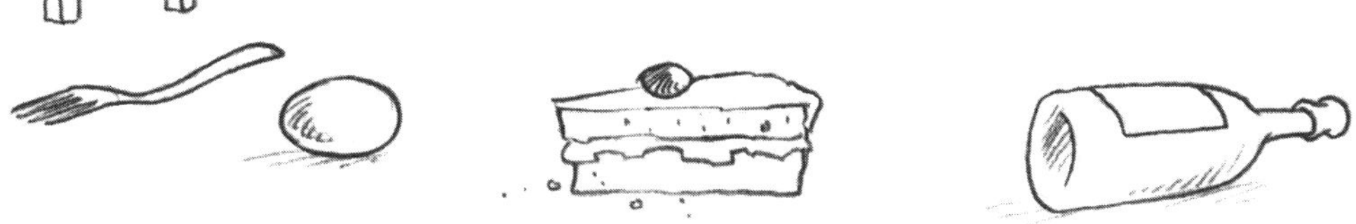

Very important words

Die kleinen Wörter in den Wolken sind sehr wichtig.

but - aber

other – andere / anderes / anderer

more - mehr

all – alles / alle

again - wieder

or - oder

only - nur

now - jetzt

some – einige / einiges

Lies die Wörter immer wieder durch,
bis du sie auswendig gelernt hast.
Welche Wolkenwörter passen in die Rahmen ?

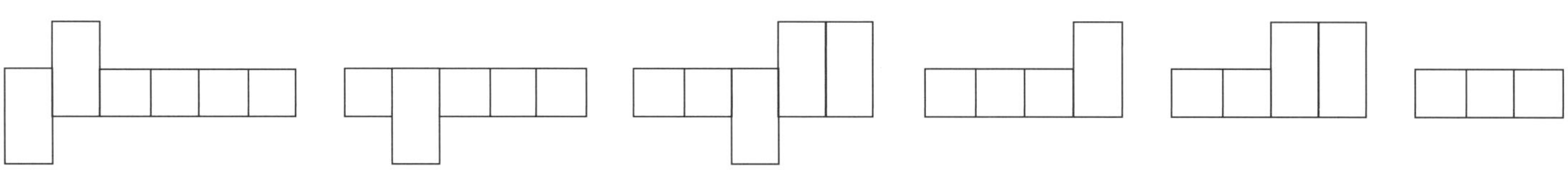

Bilde jetzt Sätze, in denen möglichst viele Wolkenwörter vorkommen. Streiche jedes Wort durch, das du in einem Satz benutzt hast!

many - viele

the same - das gleiche

please - bitte

each – jede / jeder / jedes

wrong - falsch

because - weil

if - wenn, falls

with - mit

right - richtig

Rhyme time

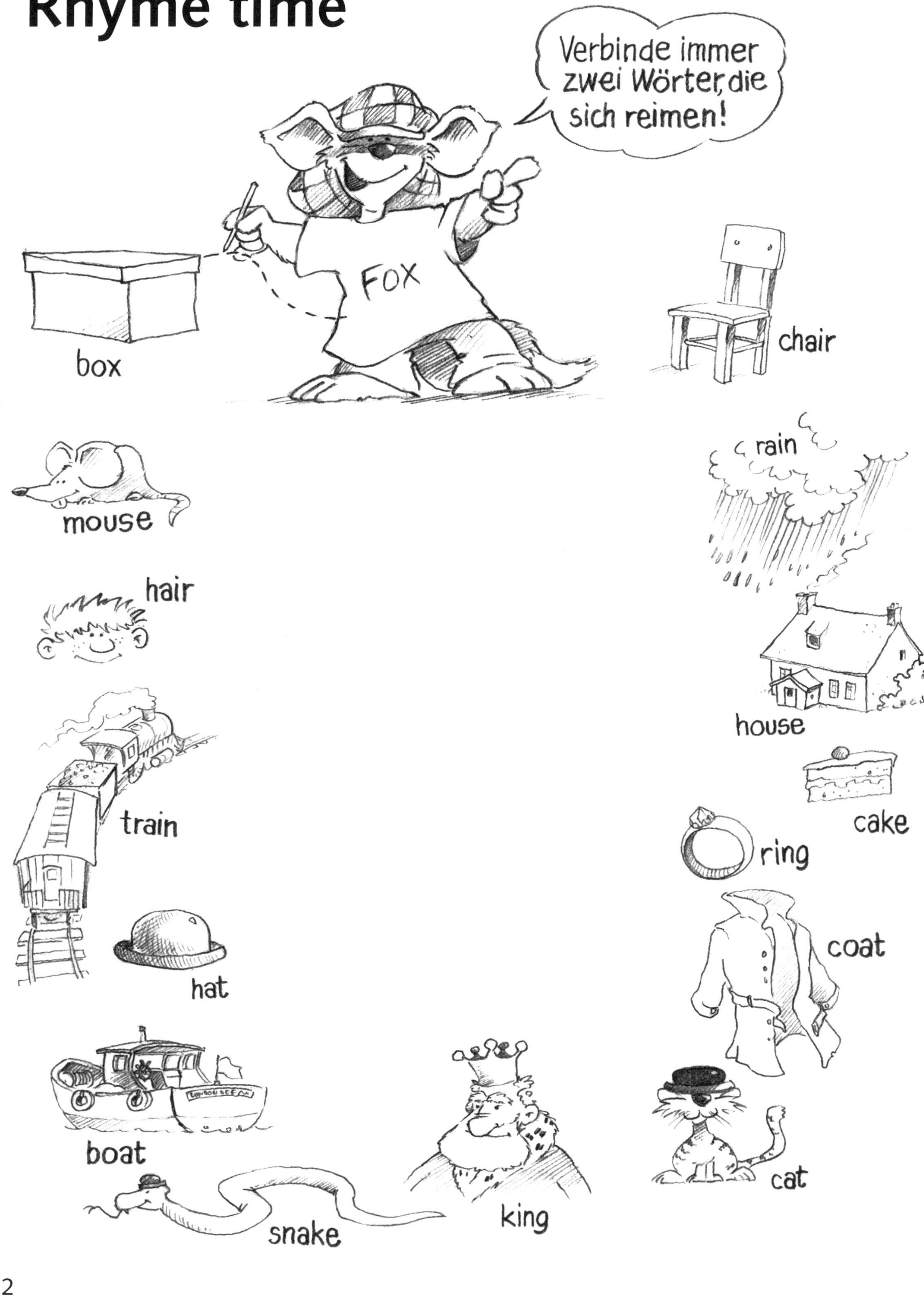
Verbinde immer zwei Wörter, die sich reimen!
FOX
box
mouse
hair
train
hat
boat
snake
king
chair
rain
house
cake
ring
coat
cat

Schreibe die Wörter auf Freddys Schild so in die leeren Kästchen, dass immer zwei Reimwörter miteinander verbunden sind.

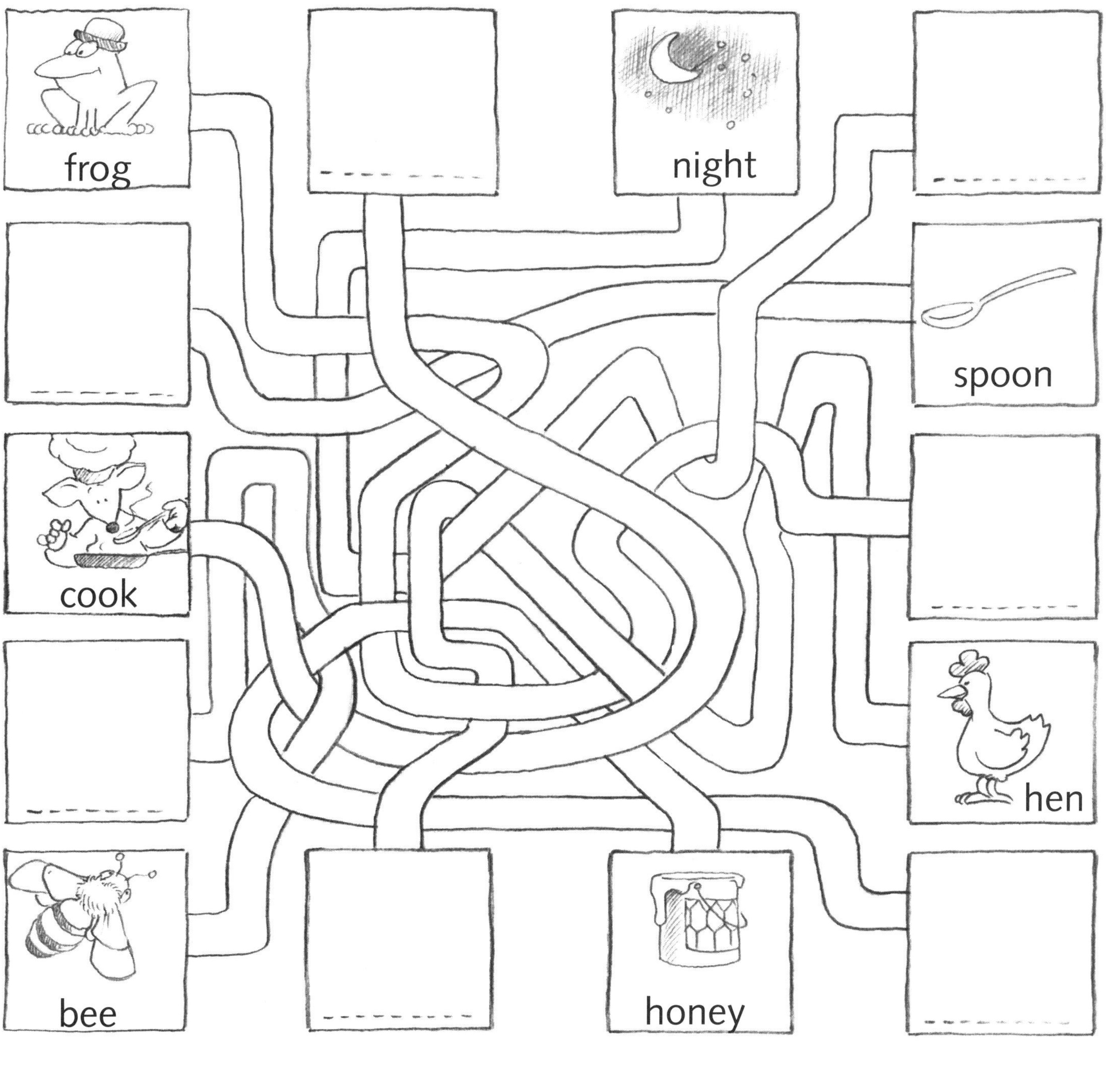

Hobbies

I like riding my bike.

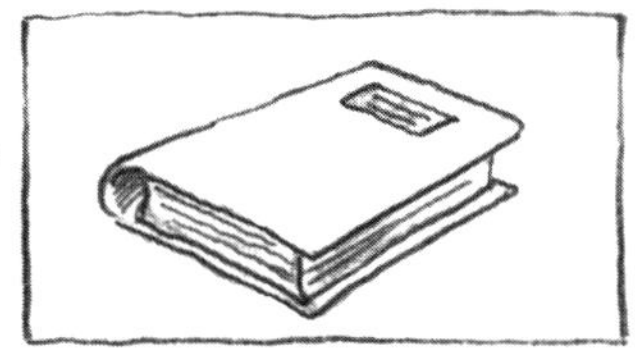

I like reading.

I like playing table-tennis.

I like playing with my doll.

I like listening to music.

I like playing computer games.

What is your hobby ?

Draw your picture here!

I like ______________________________

Opposites

Trage immer die Gegenteile der angegebenen Wörter ein!

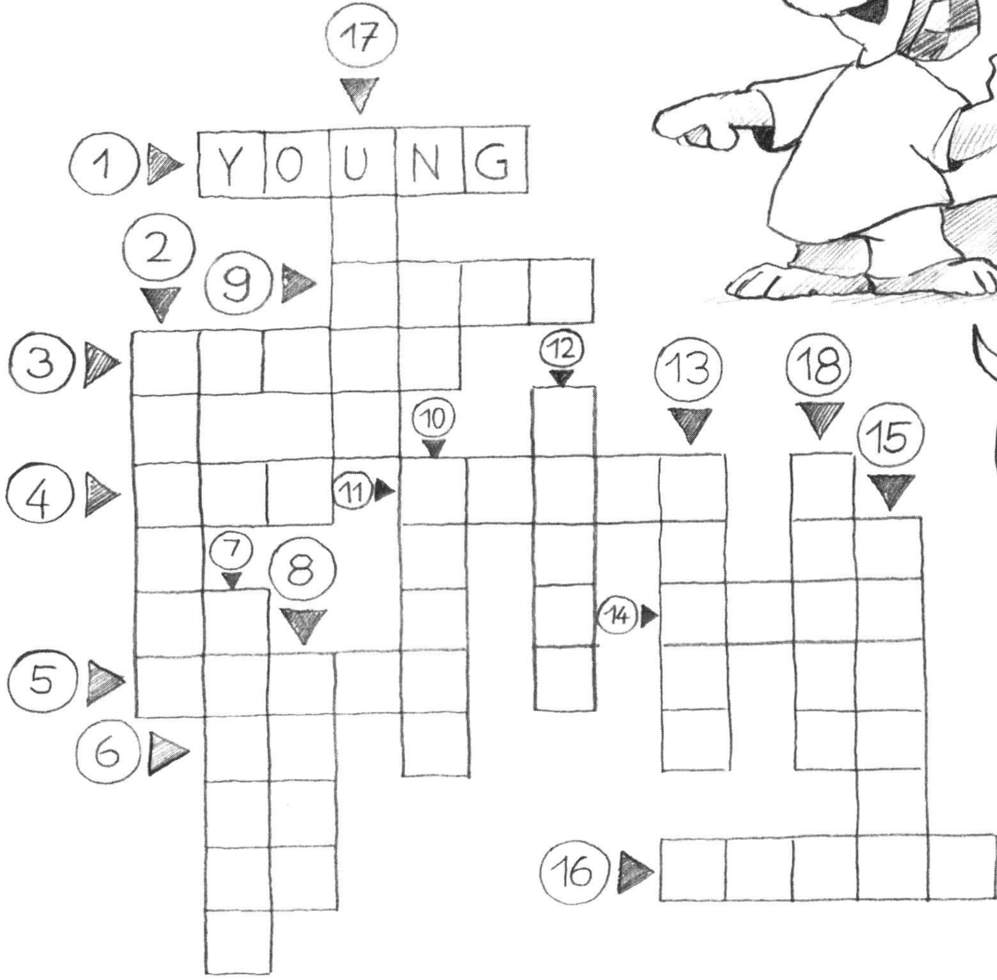

1	old	7	summer	13	day
2	question	8	bad	14	boy
3	before	9	up	15	stupid
4	happy	10	black	16	long
5	wrong	11	man	17	over
6	yes	12	full	18	last

Hier darfst du spicken:
young, answer, after, sad, right, no, winter, good, down, white, woman, empty, night, girl, clever, short, under, first

Colours

Kreuze an, welche Farbe die Tiere und Dinge haben!
Male dann bitte die Bilder in den jeweiligen Farben an!

frog

- ○ red
- ○ green
- ○ grey

sun

- ○ blue
- ○ black
- ○ yellow

tomato

- ○ red
- ○ pink
- ○ white

elephant

- ○ grey
- ○ blue
- ○ orange

pig

- ○ grey
- ○ pink
- ○ yellow

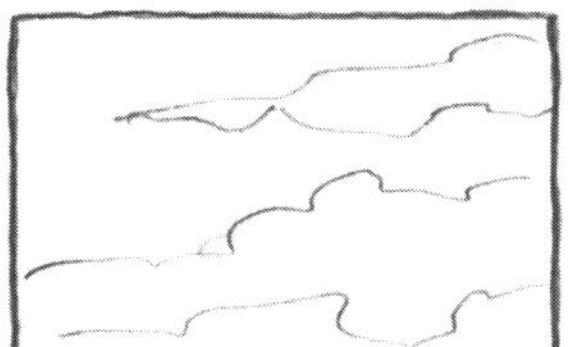
sky

- ○ brown
- ○ green
- ○ blue

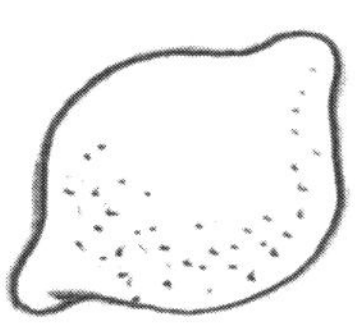
lemon

- ○ black
- ○ red
- ○ yellow

strawberry

- ○ red
- ○ blue
- ○ orange

carrot

- ○ orange
- ○ pink
- ○ blue

night

- ○ white
- ○ black
- ○ red

Verbs and nouns

Verbinde jedes Verb mit dem passenden Bild!

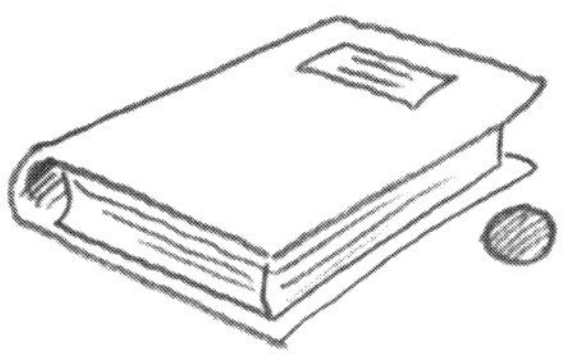
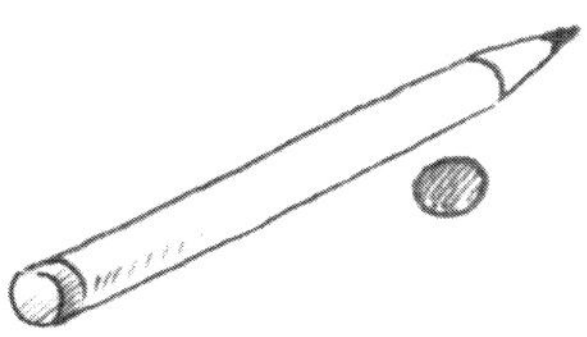

eat

drink

read

drive

sit

write

watch

sleep

play

call

clean

carry

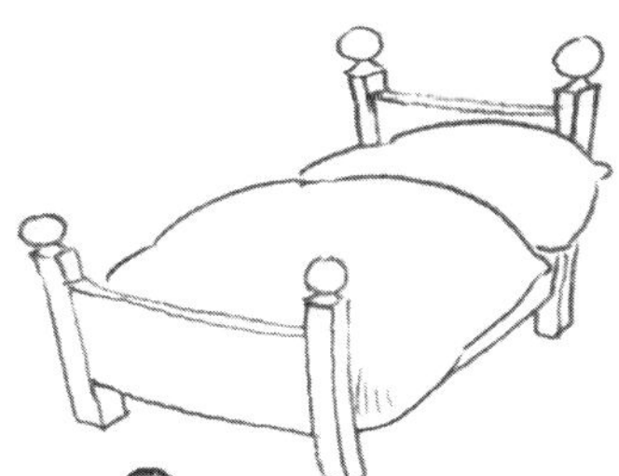

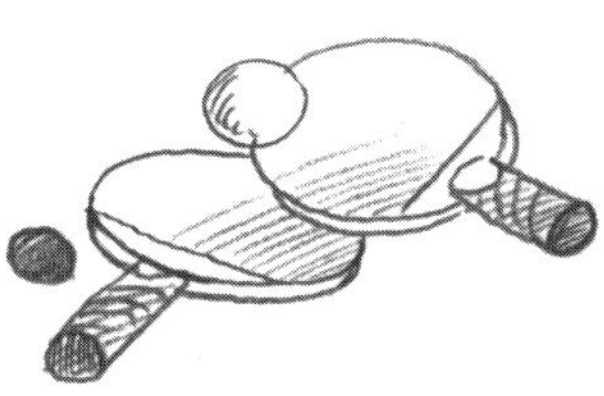

Word hunt

Suche bitte zu jedem Bild das passende Wort im Rahmen und kreise es ein!
Schreibe dann jedes Wort unter das entsprechende Bild!

cathousegirlelephantbikebook

carfoxwomanpencildoordogshirtapple

treesuncowbananaboyhandstarballwindow

bedflowerrulerbirdmanboxsatchel

Describing animals and things

Zu welchem Tier oder welchem Ding passen beide Adjektive (Eigenschaftswörter)? Kreuze an!

big & yellow

small & old

cold & wet

black & short

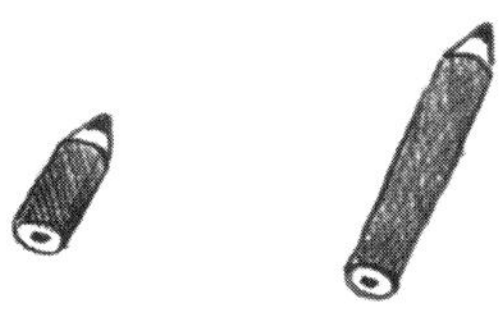

sour & yellow

cold & soft

small & grey

sweet & red

round & heavy

The broken window mystery*

Wer hat das Fenster von Richard Rabbit eingeworfen? Du bekommst es schnell heraus, wenn du in den Sätzen alle **Q**, **U** und **Z** streichst und die übrigen Buchstaben zusammen liest.

- QIUTZIQSQNZOUTZZAQPQUIUZGQ .
- ZIZTQZIUZSQNZUOTQFQRZEUDDZYQFQOZX .
- IQTQIZSSUOUMUEZONQEZQWUZIQZTUHQZ BZULUAQQZCUKUQZSQZHUZOQEQSZQU .
- QQIZTUZIQZSUUTHZQEZUOUZNQZEUZ WQQZIUZTQHQZUAZQUHQZUAQZTQ .

*mystery - Rätsel, Geheimnis

What does it say?

Lies bitte jeden Satz genau und kreuze dann das passende Bild dazu an!

Freddy reads a book.

The pigs like to dance.

Sally the mouse is cleaning her house.

The sun is behind a cloud.*

Nancy the cat buys ice cream.

Trage jetzt die Erkennungsbuchstaben der fünf angekreuzten Bilder hier ein:

!

* cloud - Wolke

Betrachte jetzt die Bilder ganz genau und kreuze die passenden Sätze an! Achtung! Manchmal können auch mehrere Sätze richtig sein.

- ○ Charly Frog sleeps in the bed. (K)
- ○ Charly Frog is swimming in the lake. (N)
- ○ Charly Frog buys ice cream. (C)

- ○ It‘s Mousy‘s birthday party. (I)
- ○ There are seven candles on the cake. (C)
- ○ Freddy is blowing out the lights. (W)

- ○ Two pigs are playing with a ball. (E)
- ○ Two pigs are playing table-tennis. (A)
- ○ Two pigs are playing outside. (J)

- ○ Freddy is drawing a bird. (L)
- ○ Freddy is drawing a house. (O)
- ○ Freddy goes fishing. (D)

- ○ Charly and Mousy listen to the music. (B)
- ○ Charly and Mousy are dancing. (O)
- ○ Freddy and Mousy are at school. (M)

Trage die Erkennungsbuchstaben der 7 angekreuzten Sätze hier ein:

								!

What doesn‘t belong?

In jeder Wörtergruppe passt ein Wort nicht dazu.
Streiche es bitte durch!
Suche dafür aus Freddys Kiste ein passendes Wort aus
und schreibe es in die leere Zeile!

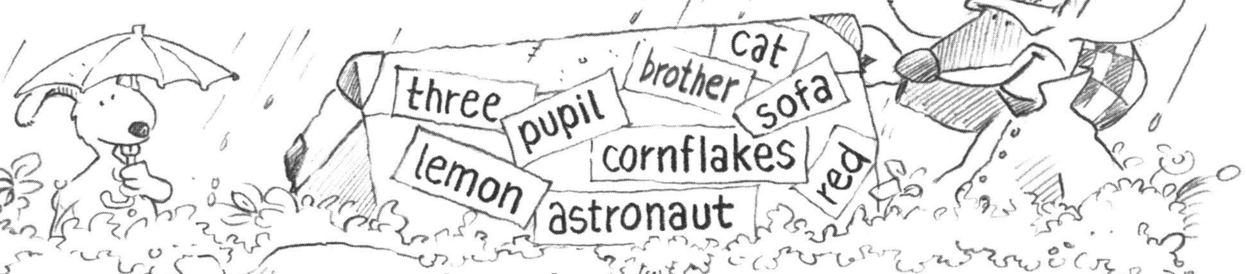

animals

- ○ fox
- ○ mouse
- ○ dog
- ○ chair
- ○

school

- ○ book
- ○ pencil
- ○ car
- ○ teacher
- ○

numbers

- ○ seven
- ○ write
- ○ two
- ○ five
- ○

colours

- ○ blue
- ○ green
- ○ yellow
- ○ four
- ○

family

- ○ sister
- ○ grandfather
- ○ camel
- ○ mother
- ○

fruits

- ○ bike
- ○ banana
- ○ apple
- ○ melon
- ○

furniture*

- ○ table
- ○ pencil
- ○ chair
- ○ cupboard
- ○

space**

- ○ rocket
- ○ moon
- ○ star
- ○ tree
- ○

food

- ○ bread
- ○ book
- ○ cheese
- ○ steak
- ○

* furniture - Möbel ** space - Weltraum

Cross one out!

In jeder Zeile passt ein Begriff
nicht zu den anderen.
Streiche ihn durch!

cat car chair house cow

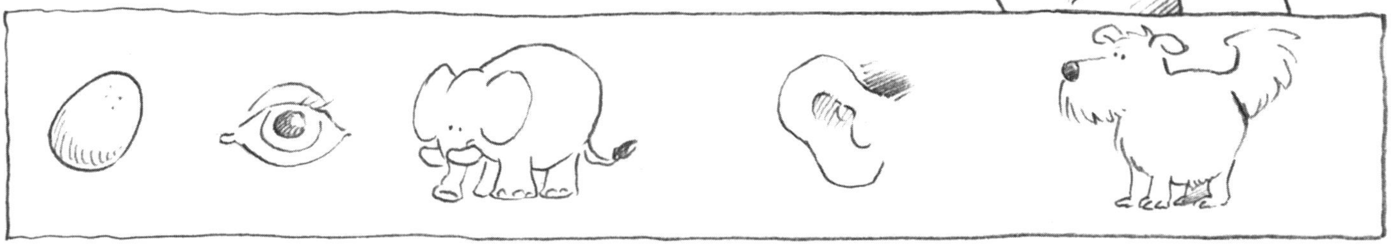

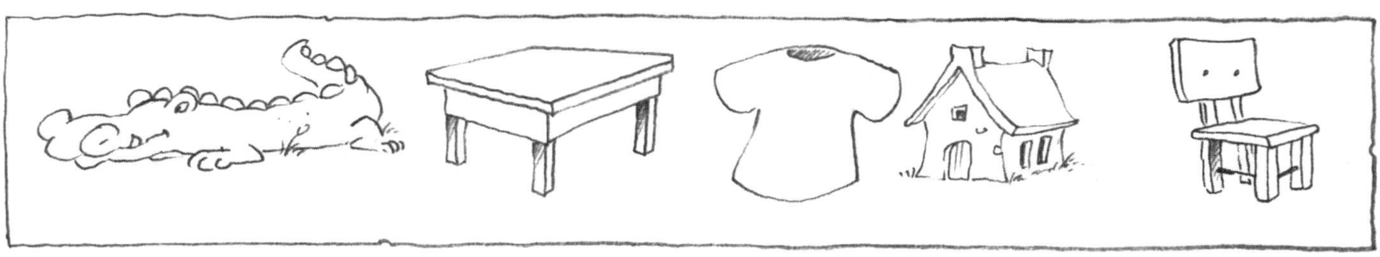

Die Auflösung findest du auf Seite 64!

Name the groups!

flowers • Blumen
food • Lebensmittel
clothes • Kleidung
fruits • Obst
insects • Insekten
toys • Spielzeug
shapes • Formen

insects	

	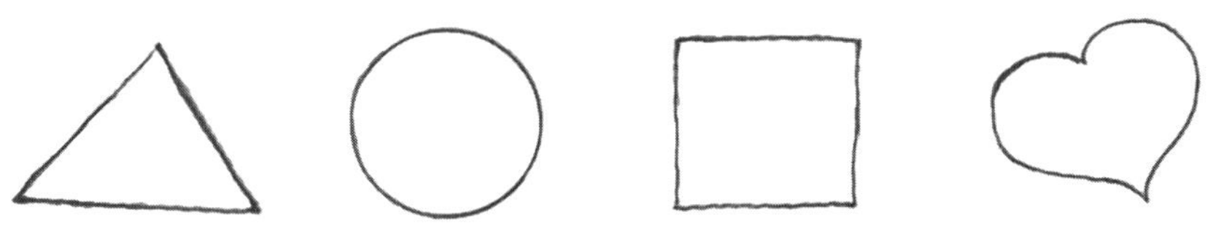

	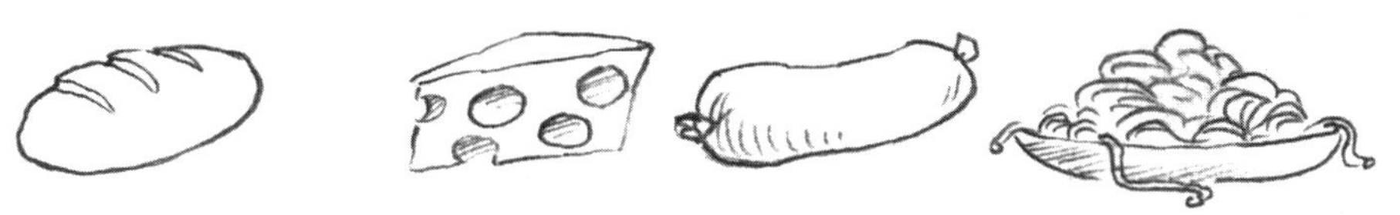

Crossword puzzle

Ordne die Buchstaben so, dass sinnvolle Wörter entstehen.
Trage die Wörter dann ins Rätselgitter ein!

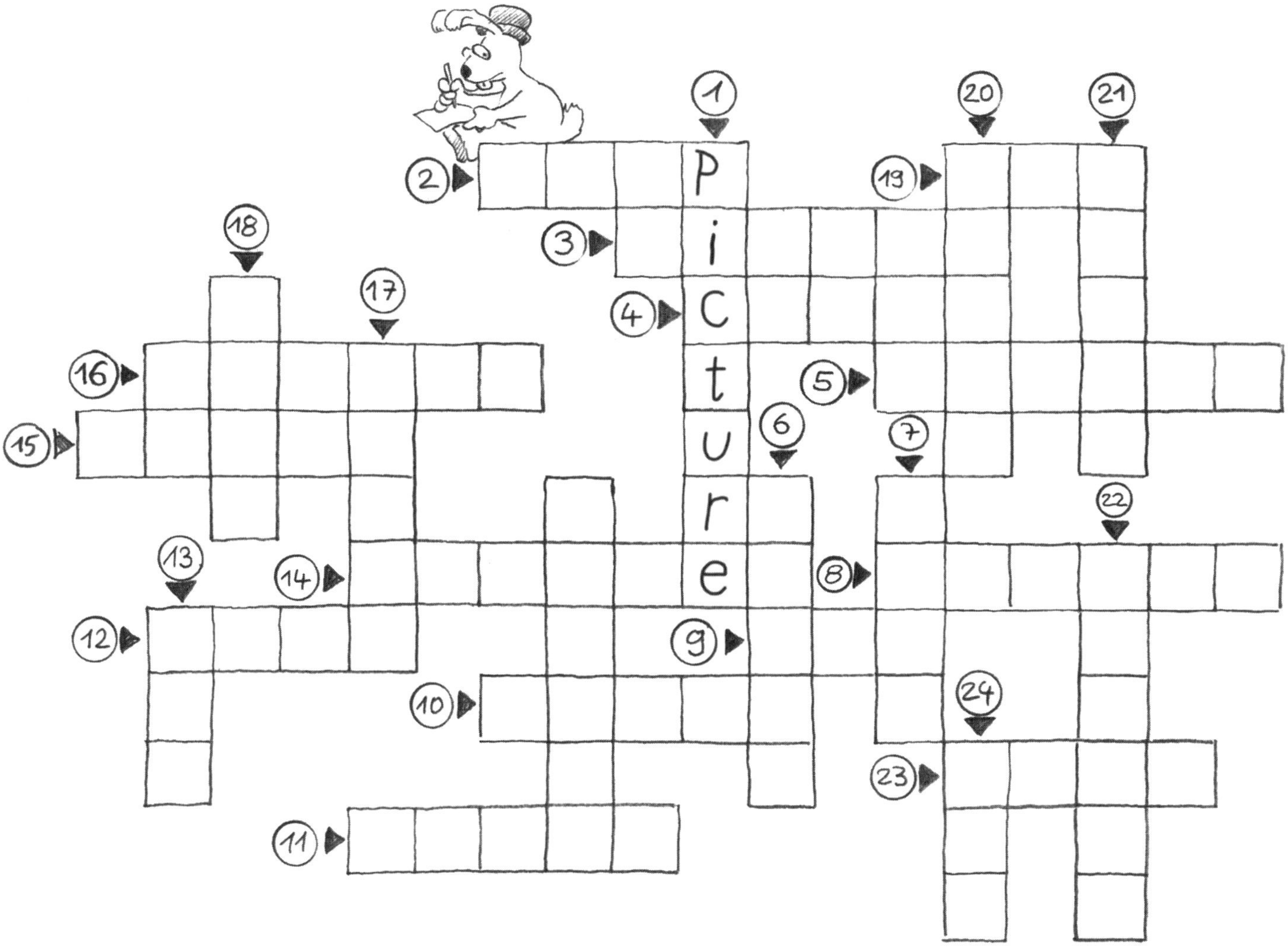

1. pctruei
2. mjup
3. wwidno
4. acr
5. welloy
6. gneer
7. teer
8. brubre
9. eey
10. ouhse
11. papel
12. ekbi
13. oxb
14. chearet
15. raich
16. wolfre
17. rwtie
18. aypl
19. tis
20. weest
21. eblta
22. ketasb
23. akce
24. tac

Let's rhyme!

Male die Luftballons, deren Wörter sich reimen, bunt aus!

Streiche bitte in jeder Reihe das Wort durch, das sich nicht auf die anderen Wörtern reimt!

hat	cat	wet	let	eight	get
tree	bee	she	knee	we	my
ball	call	full	doll	roll*	all

*roll - Brötchen

Complete!

Ergänze die fehlenden Wörter!

socks on the rocks

a cake in a _ _ _ _

a frog on a ___ ___ ___

the moon with a _ _ _ _ _

a chair with black _ _ _ _

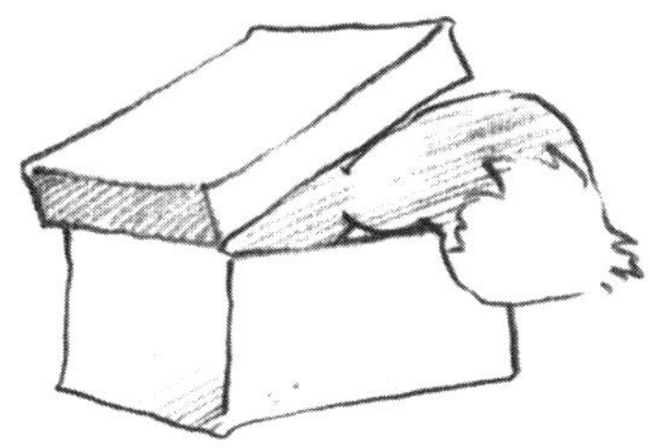

a fox in a ___ ___ ___

number „eight“ on a _ _ _ _ _

a train in the _ _ _ _

a hen with a _ _ _

The apple tree

Pflücke die Wörter vom Apfelbaum und schreibe sie auf die Körbe! Achte auf die Wortrahmen!

Days of the week

a week						
Sunday	Monday	Tuesday	Wednesday	Thursday	Friday	Saturday

Trage bitte alle Wochentage in das Rätselgitter ein!

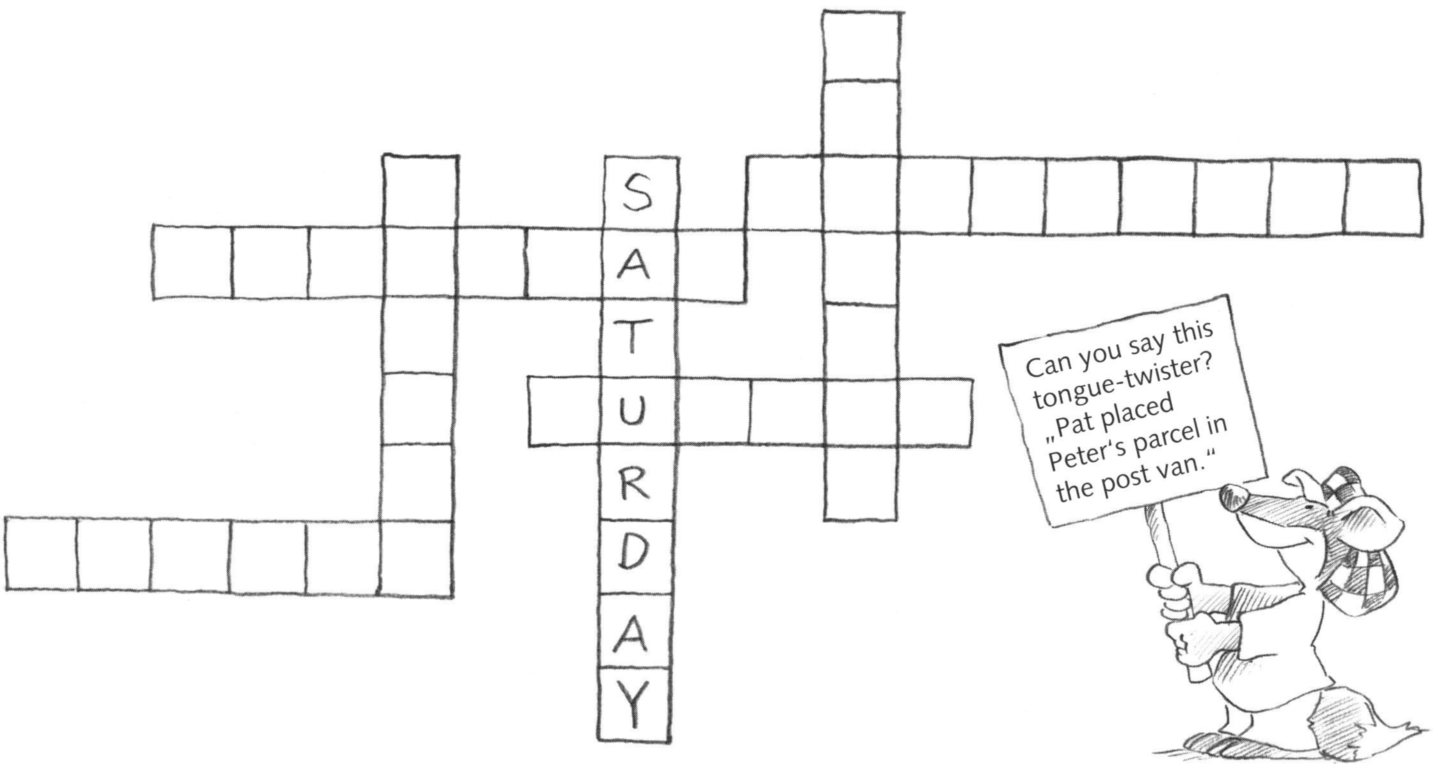

Schreibe die Lösungen neben die Rätselfragen!

★ Today is Tuesday. What was yesterday? ____________________

★ Yesterday was Friday. What will tomorrow be? ____________________

★ Today is Thursday. What was yesterday? ____________________

★ Tomorrow will be Saturday. What is today? ____________________

★ Yesterday was Monday. What is today? ____________________

★ Yesterday was Tuesday. What will tomorrow be? ____________________

★ What day is today? ____________________

★ What day was yesterday? ____________________

★ What day will tomorrow be? ____________________

What colour?

Male bitte Freddys Sachen in den vorgegebenen Farben an.
Ergänze dann die Sätze!

Freddy's	car	is	blue
Freddy's	shirt	is	______
Freddy's	cap	is	______
Freddy's	book	is	______
Freddy's	bike	is	______
______	bag	is	______
______	apple	___	______
______	kite	___	______
______	ball	___	______
______	boat	___	______
______	train	___	______
______	umbrella	___	______
______	shoes	are	______
______	shorts	___	______

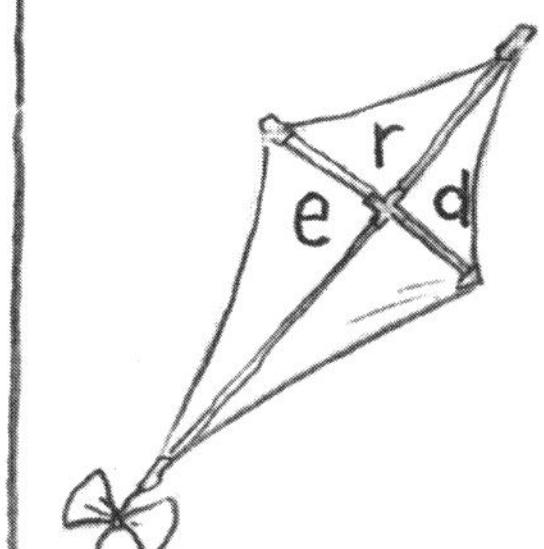

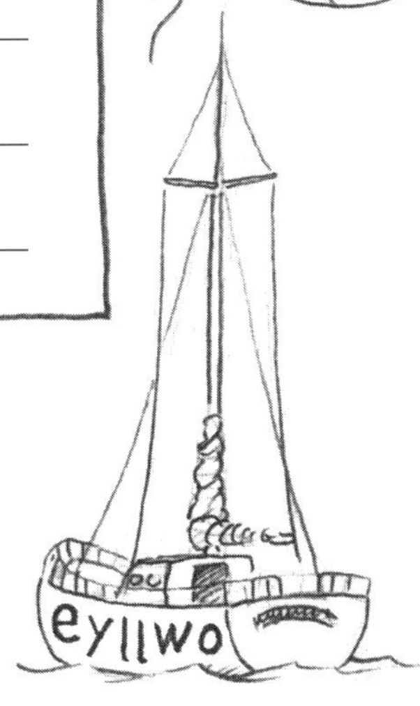

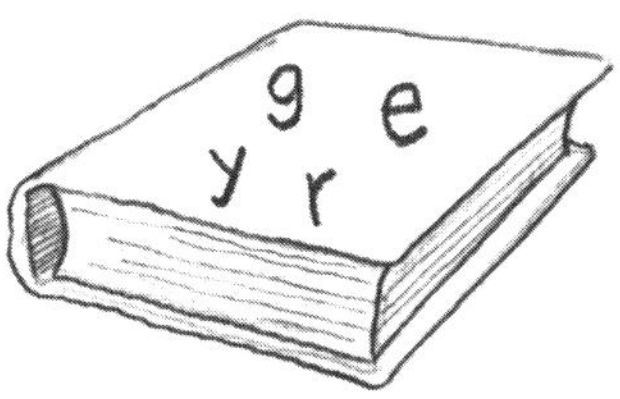

Month of the year

Spell each month of the year!
Complete the words!

J _ _ _ _ _ y

F _ _ _ _ _ _ _ _

M _ _ _ _

A _ _ _ _

M _ _

J _ _ _

J _ _ _

Au _ _ _ _ _

S _ _ _ _ _ _ _ _ _

O _ _ _ _ _ _ _

N _ _ _ _ _ _ _ _

D _ _ _ _ _ _ _ _

July March August April
January September December May
June October November February

Write the name of the month we are in now: ____________________

Write the month of your birthday: ______________________________

Memory* game

Schau die Bilder und Wörter genau an und versuche, dir so viele wie möglich einzuprägen!
Decke nach einer Minute das Bild ab und schreibe alle Begriffe, an die du dich noch erinnerst, in die Zeilen!

Wer mehr als 15 Wörter gewusst hat, ist super!
Schreibe alle fehlenden Wörter mit einem roten Stift in die Zeilen!

*memory - Gedächtnis

Pictures and Words

In jedem Kästchen gibt es nur ein Bild mit dem passenden Wort. Kreise bitte das Bild und das Wort ein!

Trage die Anfangsbuchstaben der eingekreisten Wörter der Reihe nach hier ein:

Missing letters

Ergänze bitte die fehlenden Buchstaben in den Wörtern!
Streiche die eingesetzten Buchstaben in der Leiste durch!

m
g
g
a
b
o
e
x
c
w
o
d
y
w
d
k

bo_t

plan_

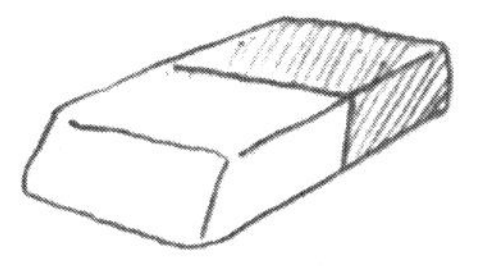

rub_er

flo_er

co_puter

villa_e

fo_

famil_

gran_father

_oman

_nife

tea_her

Trage alle übrigen Buchstaben aus der Buchstabenleiste hier ein:

!

Animals

Von welchen Tieren findest du die Umrisse im großen Bild?
Kreuze sie bitte an!

Ob du alles richtig gemacht hast, bekommst du so heraus:
Zähle die Erkennungszahlen der **8** angekreuzten Tiere zusammen!
Die Summe ist **80**!

Three - letter - words

Ergänze die fehlenden Buchstaben und verbinde jedes Wort mit dem passenden Bild:

c ow		__ ed
__ ot		__ ar
__ up		__ eg
__ ag		__ og
__ un		__ oy
__ an		__ ar
__ ox		__ gg
__ ye		__ en
__ ee		__ ey

Fun with words

Oh je, Freddy hat ja fast alles falsch gemacht! Nur auf 5 Kärtchen stimmen Bild und Wort überein. Kreuze sie bitte an!

Trage die Anfangsbuchstaben der angekreuzten Kärtchen hier ein:

!

Worm words

Male bitte jeden Buchstabenwurm in einer anderen Farbe aus! Suche dann zu den 8 Wörtern die passenden Bilder und kreuze sie an!

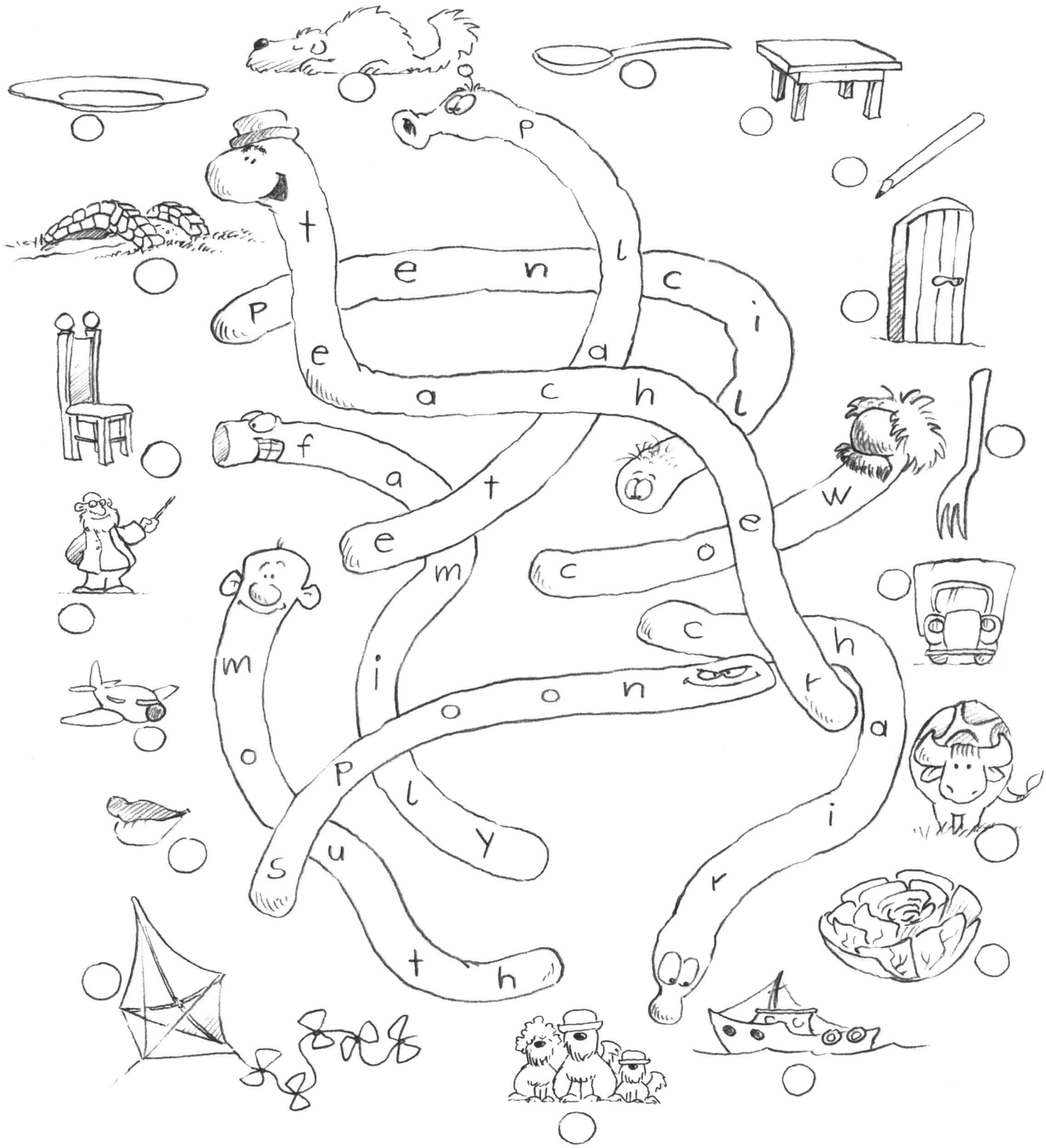

What's the time, Mr. Fox?

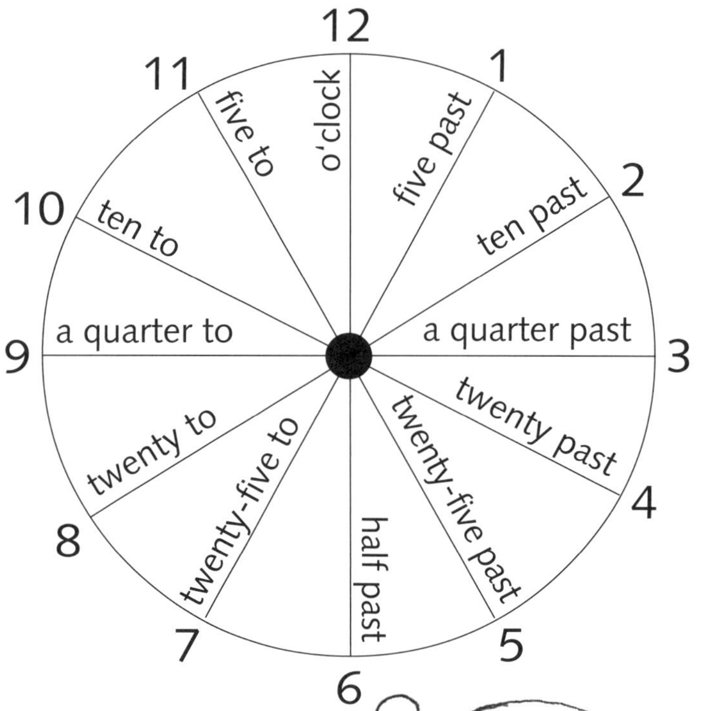

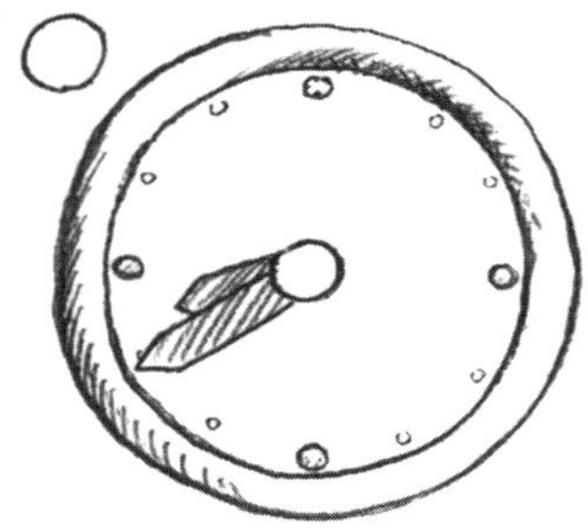

It's ten past eleven.

It's half past seven.

It's twenty to nine.

It's a quarter past one.

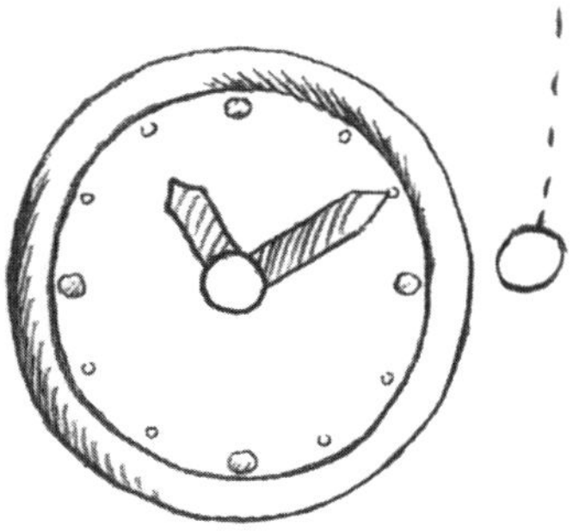

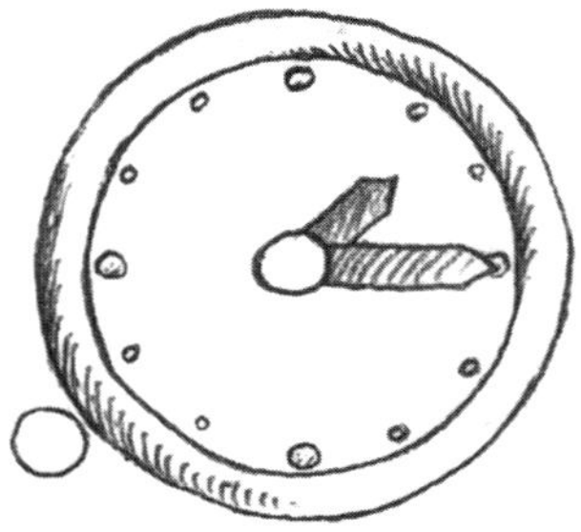

It's a quarter to four.

It's three o'clock.

It's five to ten.

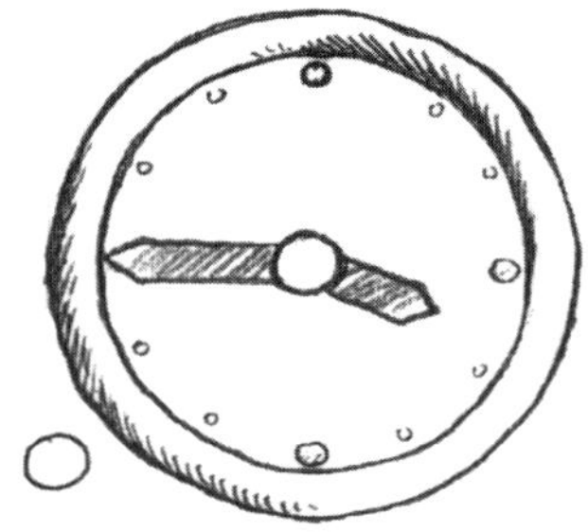

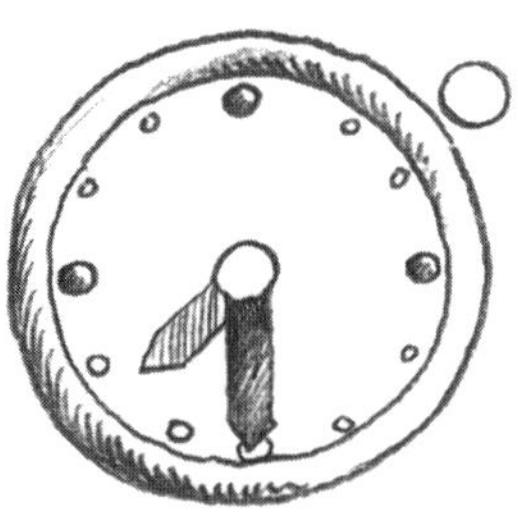

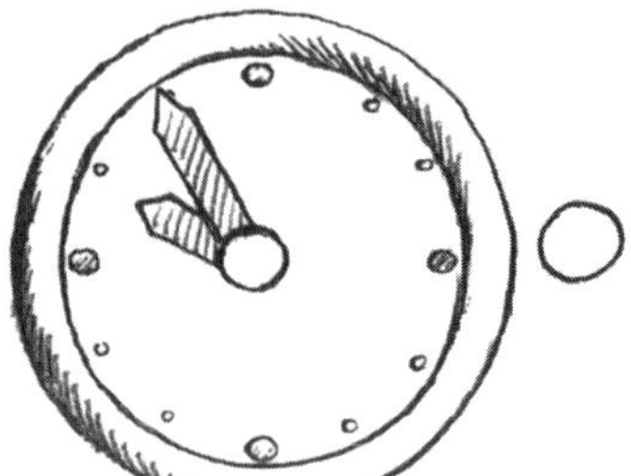

What time is it when an elephant sits on a car?

Time to buy a new car.

Find the word!

Kreuze die richtigen Wörter an!

 ○ boy ○ blue ○ boat	 ○ ear ○ eye ○ egg	 ○ car ○ cat ○ cup
 ○ lion ○ love ○ lamp	 ○ book ○ rock ○ cook	 ○ red ○ road ○ ring
 ○ winter ○ window ○ flower	 ○ boat ○ bird ○ book	 ○ ice ○ egg ○ eye
 ○ shoe ○ school ○ sock	 ○ black ○ coat ○ boat	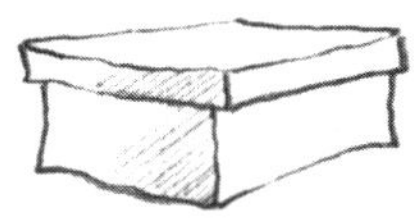 ○ box ○ fox ○ rock
 ○ car ○ but ○ bus	 ○ ring ○ run ○ roll	 ○ villa ○ village ○ van
 ○ basket ○ corn ○ bucket	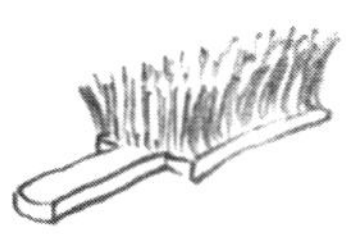 ○ bread ○ brush ○ bush	 ○ butter ○ flash ○ bottle
 ○ comb ○ camel ○ cat	 ○ fish ○ ship ○ frog	 ○ ball ○ bell ○ Billy
 ○ cheese ○ chef ○ chair	 ○ sand ○ son ○ snake	 ○ fire ○ fox ○ fly
 ○ rain ○ tray ○ train	 ○ sun ○ star ○ moon	

Broken word

Schau jedes Kästchen genau an! Male, was du siehst, in das graue Kästchen mit der gleichen Nummer!

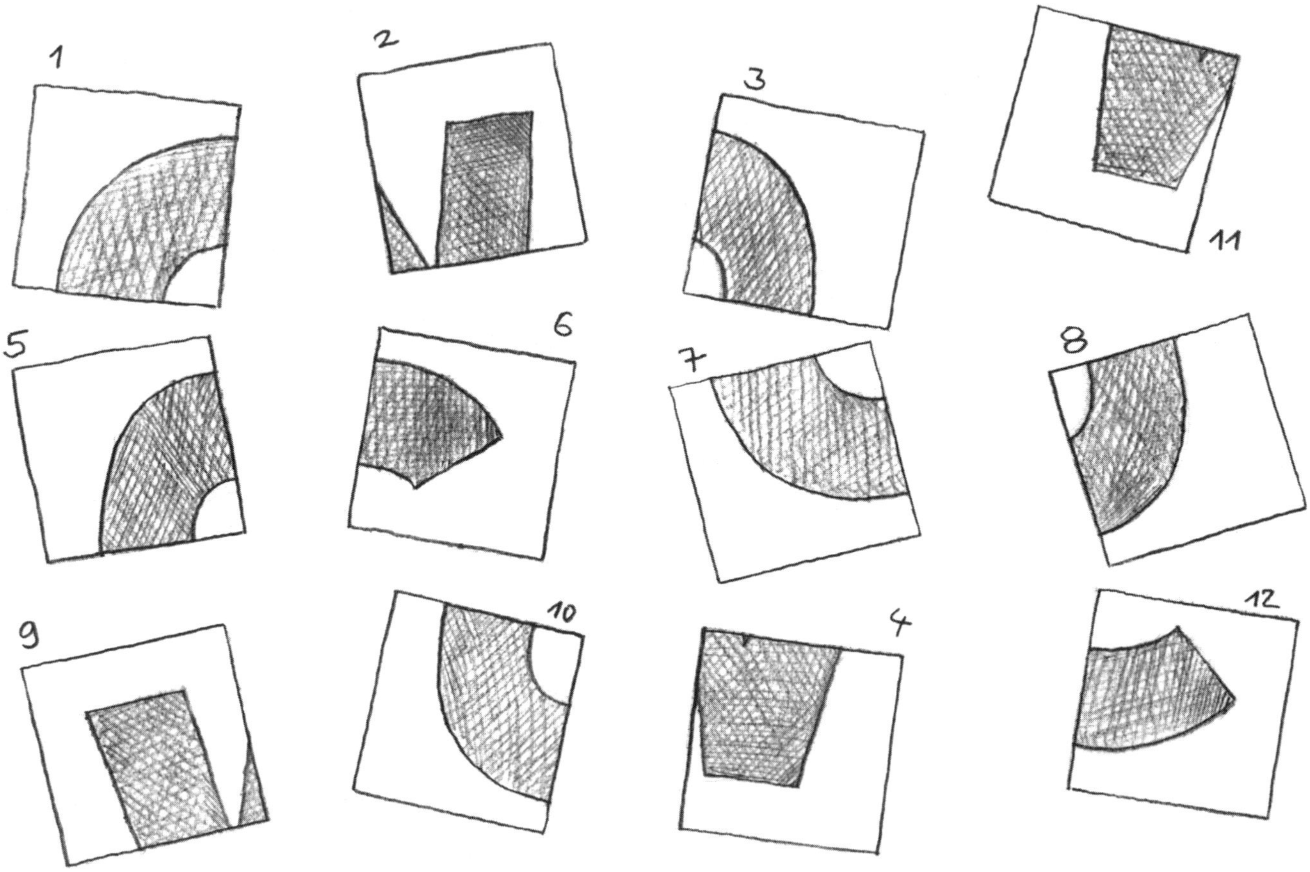

Wenn du alles richtig gemacht hast, kannst du in den grauen Kästchen einen Tiernamen lesen.
Kreuze das passende Tierbild an!

Question game

Ergänze die Fragewörter, mit denen Freddy jongliert,
in den Sätzen!
Trage dann die Nummern der passenden Antwortsätze
hinter den Fragen ein!

How old is Nancy, the cat? ◯ ______

______ time is it? ◯ ______

______ are you wearing warm clothes? ◯ ______

______ reads the newspaper? ◯ ______

______ is your little sister? ◯ ______

______ is Charly's birthday? ◯ ______

① She is in the garden.	② It's half past five.	③ Mary reads the newspaper every day.	④ Nancy is eight years old.	⑤ It's on the 5th of April.	⑥ Because it's cold outside.

Alles richtig gemacht?
Dann hast du die Zahlen in dieser Reihenfolge eingetragen:

four - two - six - three - one - five

Where are the animals?

Kreuze bitte an, wo die Tiere sind!

- behind ○
- in ○
- under ○
- on ○
- in front of ○

- behind ○
- in ○
- under ○
- on ○
- in front of ○

- behind ○
- in ○
- under ○
- on ○
- in front of ○

- behind ○
- in ○
- under ○
- on ○
- in front of ○

- behind ○
- in ○
- under ○
- on ○
- in front of ○

- behind ○
- in ○
- under ○
- on ○
- in front of ○

- behind ○
- in ○
- under ○
- on ○
- in front of ○

- behind ○
- in ○
- under ○
- on ○
- in front of ○

- behind ○
- in ○
- under ○
- on ○
- in front of ○

The treasure hunt

Freddy und seine Freunde gehen auf Schatzsuche.
In welchem Feld auf der Schatzkarte ist der Schatz versteckt?
Folge den Angaben und male ein rotes **X** in das Schatzfeld!

North - Norden	East - Osten	South - Süden	West - Westen

North

West

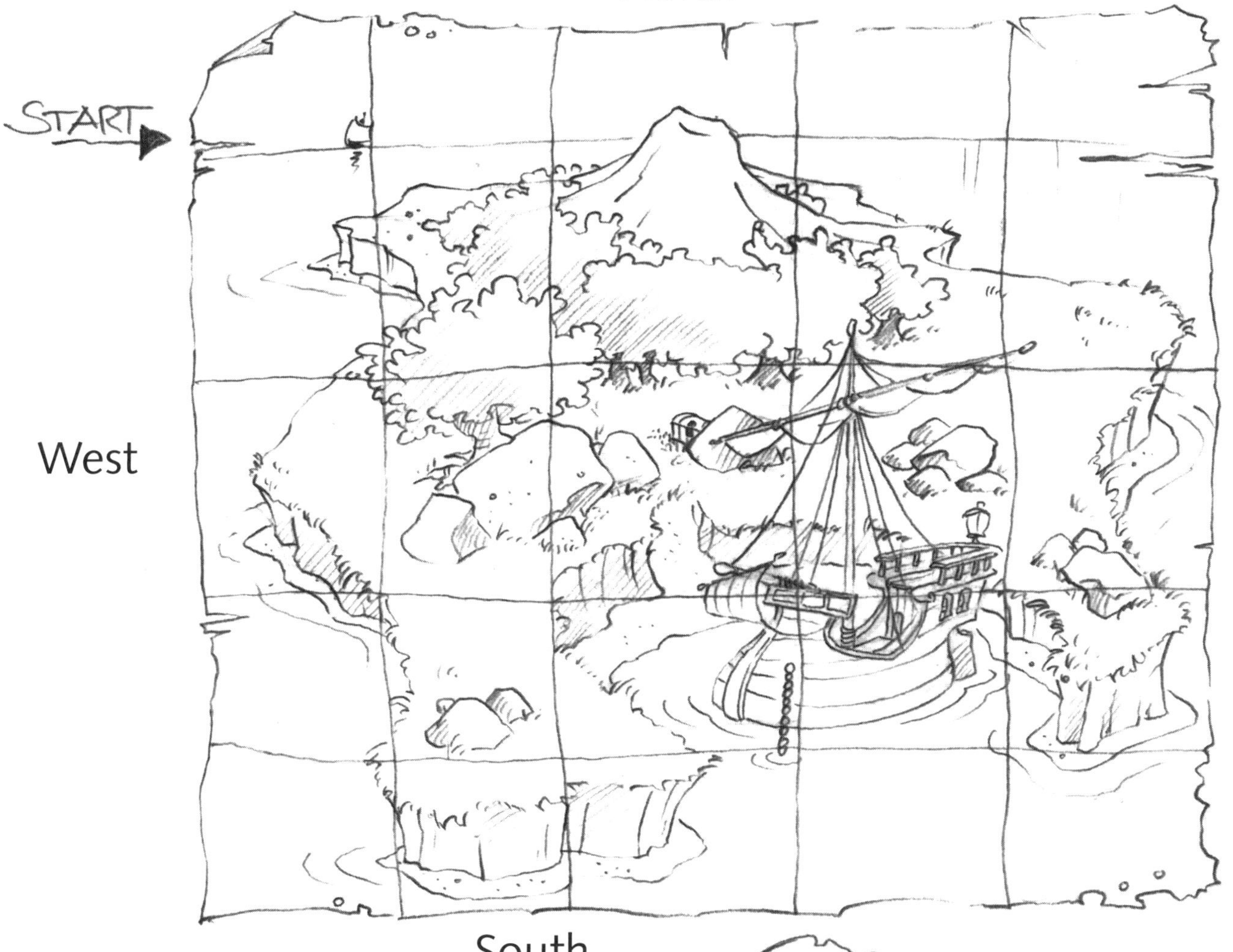

East

South

East 4
South 3
West 2
North 2
East 1
South 1

Die Freunde haben das Versteck gefunden.
Aber was ist hier eigentlich versteckt?
Folge wieder den Angaben!
Kreise die Buchstaben ein, auf die du stößt!

N

START →

D	O	M	P	A	Z	A	G
R	B	R	E	T	L	V	B
L	I	R	F	K	E	J	A
N	O	M	C	U	A	B	M
I	T	A	M	N	F	R	D
P	R	D	I	A	S	O	P
H	L	H	S	T	B	E	I
L	X	V	O	C	K	B	F

W E

S

East	7
South	3
West	5
South	4
East	2
North	5
East	4
South	3
West	7
North	3
East	5
South	3

Trage die eingekreisten Buchstaben hier ein!

What is the treasure?

Jane and Brian

Wem gehören die abgebildeten Dinge?
Schreibe die Sätze so wie im Beispiel!

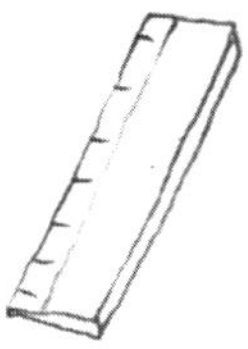

This is Jane‘s ruler.
It‘s her ruler.

This ____________________

____

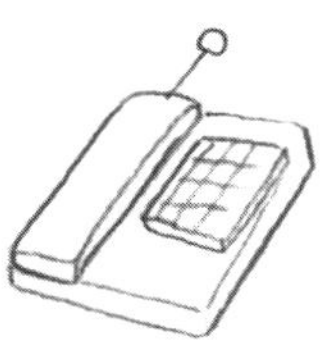

____

____

____

____

____

____

____

____

This is Brian‘s book.
It‘s his ____________

____

____

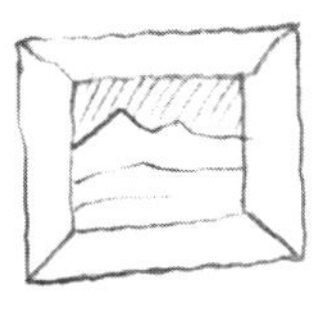

____

____

____

____

____

____

____

____

More than one

Ein Wort wird in die Mehrzahl gesetzt, indem man **s** anhängt.
Beispiel: car**s**, dog**s**, chair**s**

Endet ein Wort aber auf:
sh, ch, s oder x,
so hängt man **es** an!
Beispiel: fox**es**, bush**es**, dress**es**, church**es**

Schreibe die Wörter in der Mehrzahl auf!

box  b _ _ _ _	duck  d _ _ _ _	bush  b _ _ _ _ _	girl  g _ _ _ _
boat  b _ _ _ _	glass  g _ _ _ _ _ _	 pen p _ _ _	watch  w_ _ _ _ _ _ _
church  ch _ _ _ _ _ _	number  n _ _ _ _ _ _ _	fox  f _ _ _ _	witch  w _ _ _ _ _ _ _
window  w_ _ _ _ _ _ _	kiss  k _ _ _ _ _ _		

Can a mouse jump higher than a house?
Yes, a house can't jump.

Things to wear

Schau die Kleidungsstücke von Freddy
und seinen Freunden genau an!
Decke die Bilder dann ab!
Lies die Wörter im Kasten und streiche acht durch,
die nicht dazu passen!

blouse shirt banana dress pen hat boots tree
tiger egg coat sweater trousers bus book sock
cap scarf cup sandal rubber

Colour the stars!

Lies die Wörter in den Sternen!
Male die Sterne gelb aus, die ein Tier oder Ding im Bild benennen!

*bridge - Brücke

Lösungen

S. 5 Lösung: YOU ARE TERRIFIC!

S. 9 rot: girl, boy, mother, baby, brother
blau: tiger, cow, elephant, mouse, cat, dog
grün: book, car, table, house, chair

S. 11 Wer richtig verbunden hat, sieht einen Stern.

S. 13 Freddy träumt von:
fish, ice-cream, pizza, cake, biscuit, cornflakes,
sausage, sandwich, chocolate, banana

S. 20/21 Die Wörter in den Rahmen heißen:
please, again, right, each, with, now,
because, many, wrong, other, only, or

S. 25 1 = young, 2 = answer, 3 = after, 4 = sad, 5 = right,
6 = no, 7 = winter, 8 = good, 9 = down, 10 = white,
11 = woman, 12 = empty, 13 = night, 14 = girl,
15 = clever, 16 = short, 17 = under, 18 = first

S. 30 IT IS NOT A PIG. IT IS NOT FREDDY FOX.
IT IS SOMEONE WITH BLACK SHOES.
IT IS THE ONE WITH A HAT. ➜ Die Maus hat die Fensterscheibe auf dem Gewissen.

S.31 Lösungswort: GREAT

S. 32 Lösung: NICE JOB

S. 34 Durchzustreichen sind: das Haus, der Hund, die Sonne,
der Fisch, die Erdbeere, das Krokodil

S. 35 Dies ist die richtige Reihenfolge der Oberbegriffe:
insects, fruits, shapes, toys, clothes, food, flowers

S. 36 1 = picture, 2 = jump, 3 = window, 4 = car, 5 = yellow,
6 = green, 7 = tree, 8 = rubber, 9 = eye, 10 = house,
11 = apple, 12 = bike, 13 = box, 14 = teacher, 15 = chair,
16 = flower, 17 = write, 18 = play, 19 = sit, 20 = sweet,
21 = table, 22 = basket, 23 = cake, 24 = cat

S. 37 In den Luftballons reimt sich nicht: with, drink, bike.
In den Reihen reimt sich nicht: eight, my, full.

S. 39 Erster Sack: come, some, near, name.
Zweiter Sack: boy, day, dog, big.
Dritter Sack: eat, sit, and, not.

S. 40

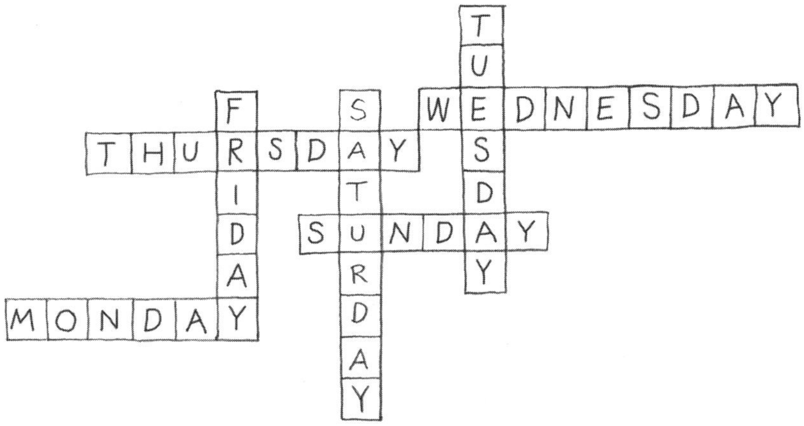

• Monday • Sunday • Wednesday • Friday • Tuesday • Thursday

S. 44 Einzukreisen war: pencil, eye, ruler, fish, elephant, cake, tree.
Lösungswort: PERFECT

S. 45 Lösungswort: GOOD

S. 48 Lösungswort: GREAT

S. 50 Die Wurmwörter heißen: teacher, plate, pencil, family, mouth, cow, chair, spoon

S. 51
1. Reihe: boy, eye, cup,
2. Reihe: lamp, book, road,
3. Reihe: window, bird, egg,
4. Reihe: shoe, boat, fox,
5. Reihe: bus, ring, village,
6. Reihe: basket, brush, bottle,
7. Reihe: camel, fish, bell,
8. Reihe: cheese, snake, fire,
9. Reihe: train, sun.

S. 52 Lösungswort: COW

S. 55 Die Schatzkiste befindet sich im mittleren Feld auf der Schatzkarte.

S. 56 Lösung: A BOX OF APPLES

S. 58 box-boxes, duck-ducks, bush-bushes, girl-girls, boat-boats, glass-glasses, pen-pens, watch-watches, church-churches, window-windows, kiss-kisses

S. 59 Im Kasten durchzustreichen war: tiger, egg, banana, pen, cup, bus, book, tree

Wörterverzeichnis Dictionary

a / an [ei, ə / æn, ən]	ein, eine, einer
about [ə'baʊt]	über (ein Thema)
after ['ɑ:ftə]	nach
again [ə'gen]	wieder
alien ['eɪljən]	Außerirdisch(er)
all [ɔ:l]	alle, alles
and [ænd, ənd]	und
angel ['eɪndʒəl]	Enge
animal ['ænɪməl]	Tier
answer ['ɑ:nsə]	Antwort
to answer [tʊ 'ɑ:nsə]	antworten
apple ['æpl]	Apfel
apple tree ['æpl tri:]	Apfelbaum
April ['eɪprəl]	April
are [ɑ:]	Form von „to be" (you are du bist, we are - wir sind)
arm [ɑ:m]	Arm
astronaut ['æstrənɔ:t]	Astronaut
August ['ɔ:gəst]	August
baby ['beɪbɪ]	Säugling, Baby
bad [bæd]	schlecht
bag [bæg]	Tasche
ball [bɔ:l]	Ball
banana [bə'nɑ:nə]	Banane
basket ['bɑ:skɪt]	Korb
bathroom ['bɑ:θrum]	Badezimmer
to be [tʊ bi:, bi]	sein
bear [bɛə]	Bär
because [bɪ'kɔz]	weil
bed [bed]	Bett
bedroom ['bedrum]	Schlafzimmer
bee [bi:]	Biene
behind [bɪ'haind]	hinter
bell [bɛl]	Glocke
to belong [tʊ bi'lɔŋ]	gehören
between [bɪ'twi:n]	zwischen
big [big]	groß
bike [baɪk]	Fahrrad
bird [bɛ:d]	Vogel
birthday ['bɜ:θdeɪ]	Geburtstag
biscuit ['bɪskɪt]	Keks
black [blæk]	schwarz
to blow [tʊ bləʊ]	pusten, wehen
to blow out [tʊ bləʊ aʊt]	auspusten
blue [blu:]	blau
boat [bəʊt]	Boot
body ['bɒdɪ]	Körper
book [bʊk]	Buch
boots [bu:ts]	Stiefel
bottle ['bɒtl]	Flasche
box [bɒks]	Schachtel
a box of...[ei, ə bɒks əv...]	eine Schachtel
boy [bɔɪ]	Junge
bread [bred]	Brot
bridge [brɪdʒ]	Brücke
to bring [tʊ brɪŋ]	bringen
broken ['brəʊkən]	zerbrochen
brother ['brʌðə]	Bruder
brown [braʊn]	braun
brush [brʌʃ]	Bürste
bucket ['bʌkɪt]	Eimer
bus [bʌs]	Bus
but [bʌt]	aber
butter ['bʌtə]	Butter
to buy [tʊ baɪ]	kaufen
bye-bye ['baɪbai]	tschüß
cake [keɪk]	Kuchen
to call [tʊ kɔ:l]	rufen
camel ['kæml]	Kamel
camera ['kæmərə]	Kamera, Fotoapparat
can ['kæn]	können
candle ['kændl]	Kerze
cap [kæp]	Kappe, Schirmmütze
car [kɑ:]	Auto
carpet ['kɑ:pɪt]	Teppich
carrot ['kærət]	Karotte
to carry [tʊ 'kærɪ]	tragen
cat [kæt]	Katze
chair [tʃeə]	Stuhl
cheese [tʃi:z]	Käse
chef [ʃef]	Chef
chocolate ['tʃɒkələt]	Schokolade
church [tʃɜ:tʃ]	Kirche
to clean [tʊ kli:n]	saubermachen, putzen
clever ['klevə]	schlau
o'clock [ə'klɒk]	Uhr (three o'clock = drei Uhr)
clothes [kləʊðz]	Kleidung
cloud [klaʊd]	Wolke
clown [klaʊn]	Clown
coat [kəʊt]	Mantel
Coke [kəʊk]	Cola
cold [kəʊld]	kalt
colour ['kʌlə]	Farbe
to colour [tʊ 'kʌlə]	anmalen
comb [kəʊm]	Kamm
to complete [tʊ kəm'pli:t]	vervollständigen
compound word [kəm'paʊnd]	zusammengesetztes Wort
computer [kəm'pju:tə]	Computer
to connect [kə'nekt]	verbinden
cook [kʊk]	Koch
to cook [tʊ kʊk]	kochen
corn [kɔ:n]	Mais
cornflakes ['kɔ:nfleɪk]	Frühstücksflocken
cow [kaʊ]	Kuh
crocodile ['krʊkədaɪl]	Krokodil
to cross out [tʊ krɒs aʊt]	ausschließen, ausstreichen, durchstreichen
crossword-puzzle ['krɒswɜ:d 'pʌzl]	Kreuzworträtsel
cup [kʌp]	Tasse
cupboard ['kʌbəd]	Küchenschrank
curtain ['kɜ:tn]	Vorhang
to dance [tʊ dɑ:ns]	tanzen
day [deɪ]	Tag
December [dɪ'sembə]	Dezember
to describe [tʊ dɪ'skraɪb]	beschreiben
to do [tʊ du:]	tun
doctor ['dɒktə]	Doktor
dog [dɒg]	Hund
doll [dɒl]	Puppe
don't (do not) [dəʊnt]	nicht tun (don't laugh = lach nicht)
door [dɔ:]	Tür
down [daʊn]	nieder
to draw [tʊ drɔ:]	zeichnen
dress [dres]	Kleid
drink [drɪŋk]	Getränk
to drink [tʊ drɪŋk]	trinken
to drive [tʊ draɪv]	fahren
duck [dʌk]	Ente
each [i:tʃ]	jede, jeder, jedes
ear [ɪə]	Ohr
east [i:st]	Osten
to eat [tʊ i:t]	essen
egg [eg]	Ei
eight [eɪt]	acht
elbow ['elbəʊ]	Ellbogen
elephant ['elɪfənt]	Elefant
eleven [ɪ'levn]	elf
empty ['emptɪ]	leer
in English [ɪn 'ɪŋglɪʃ]	auf englisch
envelope ['envələʊp]	Briefumschlag
eye [aɪ]	Auge
family ['fæməlɪ]	Familie
favourite ['feɪvərɪt]	Lieblings-... favourite colour =Lieblingsfarbe
February ['februərɪ]	Februar
finger ['fɪŋgə]	Finger
finger prints ['fɪŋgə prɪnts]	Fingerabdrücke
fire ['faɪə]	Feuer
first [fɜ:st]	erst, zuerst
fish [fɪʃ]	Fisch
five [faɪv]	fünf
flower [flaʊə]	Blume
to fly [tʊ flaɪ]	fliegen
food [fu:d]	Essen
foot / feet [fʊt / fi:t]	Fuß / Füße
to forget [tʊ fə'get]	vergessen
fork [fɔ:k]	Gabel
four [fɔ:]	vier
fox [fɒks]	Fuchs
Friday ['fraɪdɪ]	Freitag
fridge [frɪdʒ]	Kühlschrank
friend [frend]	Freund
frog [frɒg]	Frosch

fruit [fru:t]	Frucht
full [fʊl]	voll
fun [fʌn]	Spaß
furniture ['fɜ:nɪtʃə]	Möbel
game [geɪm]	Spiel
garage ['gærɑ:dʒ]	Garage
garden ['gɑ:dn]	Garten
German ['dʒɜ:mən]	deutsch, Deutsch(e, er, es)
in German [ɪn 'dʒɜ:mən]	auf deutsch
Germany ['dʒɜ:mənɪ]	Deutschland
to get [tʊ get]	bekommen
giraffe [dzɪ'rɑ:f]	Giraffe
girl [gɜ:l]	Mädchen
glass [glɑ:s]	Glas
glove [glʌv]	Handschuh
to go [tʊ gəʊ]	gehen
good [gʊd]	gut
good bye [gʊd'baɪ]	auf Wiedersehen
grandfather ['grændfɑ:ðə]	Großvater
great [greɪt]	großartig
green [gri:n]	grün
grey [greɪ]	grau

hair [heə]	Haar
half past [hɑ:f pɑ:st]	halb ... (Uhrzeit), z. B.
half past three [hɑ:f pɑ:st θri:]	halb vier
hammer ['hæmə]	Hammer
hand [hænd]	Hand
happy ['hæpɪ]	glücklich
hat [hæt]	Hut
heavy ['hevɪ]	schwer
hen [hen]	Henne, Huhn
here [hɪə]	hier
him [hɪm]	ihn, ihm
hobby / hobbies ['hɒbɪ / 'hɒbɪs]	Freizeitbeschäftigung(en)
at home [æt həʊm]	zu Hause
honey ['hʌnɪ]	Honig
horse [hɔ:s]	Pferd
hotel [həʊ'tel]	Hotel
hour ['ɑʊə]	Stunde
per hour [pə 'ɑʊə]	pro Stunde
house [hɑʊs]	Haus
how [hɑʊ]	wie
hungry ['hʌŋgrɪ]	hungrig
hunt [hʌnt]	Jagd
to hunt [tʊ hʌnt]	jagen
ice-cream ['ɑɪskri:m]	(Speise-) Eis
if [ɪf]	falls, wenn
important [ɪm'pɔ:tnt]	wichtig
in [ɪn]	in
in front of [ɪn frʌnt ɑv]	vor
insect ['ɪnsekt]	Insekt
it's (it is) [ɪts]	es ist
January ['dʒænjʊərɪ]	Januar
job [dʒɑb]	Arbeit
to join [tʊ dʒɔn]	beitreten, mitmachen
July [dʒu:'lɑɪ]	Juli
to jump [tʊ dʒʌmp]	springen
June [dʒu:n]	Juni
kids [kɪds]	Kinder
king [kɪŋ]	König
kiss [kɪs]	Kuss
to kiss [tʊ kɪs]	küssen
kitchen ['kɪtʃɪn]	Küche
kite [kɑɪt]	Drachen
knee [ni:]	Knie
knife [nɑɪf]	Messer
lamp [læmp]	Lampe
last [lɑ:st]	letzt(e, er, es)
later ['leɪtə]	später
to laugh [tʊ lɑ:f]	lachen
leg [leg]	Bein
lemon ['lemən]	Zitrone
to let [tʊ let]	lassen
letter ['letə]	Brief
light [lɑɪt]	Licht
to like [tʊ lɑɪk]	mögen
lion ['lɑɪən]	Löwe
to listen [tʊ 'lɪsn]	zuhören
little ['lɪtl]	klein
long [lɔŋ]	lang
love [lʌv]	Liebe
to love [tʊ lʌv]	lieben
to make [tʊ meɪk]	machen

man / men [mæn / men]	Mann / Männer
many ['menɪ]	viele
March [mɑ:tʃ]	März
May [meɪ]	Mai
meal [mi:l]	Mahl(zeit)
melon ['meln]	Melone
memory ['memərɪ]	Gedächtnis
mile [maɪl]	Meile
milk [mɪlk]	Milch
Monday ['mʌndɪ]	Montag
money ['mʌnɪ]	Geld
month [mʌnθ]	Monat
moon [mu:n]	Mond
moonlight ['mu:nlaɪt]	Mondschein
more [mɔ:]	mehr
more than ['mɔ: ðən]	mehr als
mother ['mʌðə]	Mutter
mouse [mɑʊs]	Maus
mouth [mɑʊθ]	Mund
music ['mju:zɪc]	Musik
my [maɪ]	mein
mystery ['mɪstərɪ]	Rätsel, Geheimnis
name [neɪm]	Name
to name [tʊ neɪm]	benennen
near [nɪə]	nahe
neck [nek]	Nacken, Hals
newspaper ['nju:speɪpə]	Zeitung
next [nekst]	(als) Nächstes; der, die, das Nächste
nice [nɑɪs]	schön
nice job! [nɑɪs dʒɔb]	gut gemacht
night [nɑɪt]	Nacht
nine [nɑɪn]	neun
no [nəʊ]	nein
north [nɔ:θ]	Norden
nose [nəʊz]	Nase
not [nɒt]	nicht
noun [nɑʊn]	Hauptwort
November [nəʊ'vembə]	November
now [nɑʊ]	jetzt
number ['nʌmbə]	Nummer

October [ok'təʊbə]	Oktober
old [əʊld]	alt
on [ɒn]	auf
one [wʌn]	eins
only ['əʊnlɪ]	nur, einzig
opposite ['ɒpəzɪt]	Gegenteil
the opposite of [ði: 'ɒpəzɪt ɑv]	das Gegenteil von
orange [ɒrɪndʒ]	orange (farben)
order ['ɔ:də]	Reihenfolge
other ['ʌðə]	ander(e, er, es)
outside [ɑʊt'saɪd]	draußen
over ['əʊvə]	über
owl [ɑʊl]	Eule
part [pɑ:t]	Teil
party ['pɑ:tɪ]	Party, Feier, Fest
past [pɑ:st]	nach
pen [pen]	Füller
pencil ['pensl]	Bleistift
penguin ['peŋgwɪn]	Pinguin
perfect ['pɜ:fɪkt]	perfekt
person ['pɜ:sn]	Person
picture ['pɪktʃə]	Bild
pig [pɪg]	Schwein
pink [pɪŋk]	rosa
pizza ['pi:tsə]	Pizza
plane [pleɪn]	Flugzeug
plate [pleɪt]	Teller
to play [tʊ pleɪ]	spielen
please [plɪ:z]	bitte
postman ['pəʊstmæn]	Briefträger
post-office ['pəʊstɑfɪs]	Postamt
pot [pɒt]	Tasse
pupil [pju:pl]	Schüler(in)
to puzzle [tʊ 'pʌzl]	puzzlen, rätseln
a quarter [ə 'kwɔ:tə]	ein Viertel
question ['kwestʃən]	Frage
rabbit ['ræbɪt]	Kaninchen, Hase
radio ['reɪdiəʊ]	Radio
rain [reɪn]	Regen
to read [tʊ ri:d]	lesen
really ['rɪəlɪ]	wirklich
red [red]	rot
restaurant ['rɛstərənt]	Restaurant, Speisegaststätte
to rhyme [tʊ rɑɪm]	reimen